Publisher's Note

The book descriptions we ask book-sellers to display prominently warn that this is an historic book with numerous typos, missing text or index and is not illustrated.

We scanned this book using character recognition software that includes an automated spell check. Our software is 99 percent accurate if the book is in good condition. However, we do understand that even one percent can be a very annoying number of typos! And sometimes all or part of a page is missing from our copy of a book. Or the paper may be so discolored from age that you can no longer read the type. Please accept our sincere apologies.

After we re-typeset and design a book, the page numbers change so the old index and table of contents no longer work. Therefore, we usually remove them.

Our books sell so few copies that you would have to pay hundreds of dollars to cover the cost of proof reading and fixing the typos, missing text and index. Therefore, whenever possible, we let our customers download a free copy of the original typo-free scanned book. Simply enter the barcode number from the back cover of the paperback in the Free Book form at www.general-books. net. You may also qualify for a free trial membership in our book club to download up to four books for free. Simply enter the barcode number from the back cover onto the membership form on the same page. The book club entitles you to select from more than a million books at no additional charge. Simply enter the title or subject onto the search form to find the books.

If you have any questions, could you please be so kind as to consult our Frequently Asked Questions page at www. general-books.net/faqs.cfm? You are also welcome to contact us there.
General Books LLC™, Memphis, USA, 2012.

❧ ❧ ❧ ❧ ❧ ❧ ❧ ❧

THE NEW SCIENCE OF COLOR CHAPTER I
THE NECESSITY FOR A COLOR THEATER AND COLOR COLLEGE

Since our planet stands at an unparalleled crisis in the history of her evolution, and while we are in the midst of such disruption and chaos, it may seem premature to press the claims of a new science.

Yet it is this universal passing of things that is clearing the ground for fresh growth, and no moment could be more fitting in which to herald the light that lies ahead. Therefore, before dealing directly with my subject, I will endeavor to indicate its exact relation to existing events, and to show that color-science is only the natural and necessary answer to many present needs.

No one can deny that old strictures are breaking, and obstructive conventions of thought are being scattered like dust upon the wind. Our mental and spiritual stature are on the increase, and they demand fresh vision and fresh outlets.

War has unfurled a banner in which the countries of the world are but fluttering streamers blown by the breath of one purpose—Progress.

The foundations of existence are shaking, the present and the future are filled with menace and with hope, for two cries hurtle in the air! One affirms that might is embodied in material forces; the other, that in spiritual convictions lie the true source of our strength.

For centuries man has evolved through the creation and the understanding of form; but he has now reached a point at which he is in danger of exalting the mechanism above the mind that made it, and of succumbing to an obsession of individual power.

We find, therefore, that these contradictory clamors which constitute the underlying impetus of the War are merged in one metallic protest, and that the mineral kingdom, so long wrested by man to his own service, has now reared itself against him, destructive and demand... The growing lust for wealth and the arrogance of intellectual achievement are alike finding their retribution in this chastening crisis.

The present loss of life, expenditure of money, and destruction of property compel man to realize that such things are only puppets in the pageant of evolution and not in themselves an end or a permanent possession.

Iron, copper, steel, silver and gold in various graven images of man's making are now molten to so many veins in a devouring monster that challenges the race to a conquest vaster than any it has yet known, namely, the negation of form and the triumphant declaration that it is not the visible but the invisible that counts. Surely this is the ethical significance of the world struggle now at stake.

Lust and rapine, together with all the contrivances of man, mingle chaotic in their denunciation of Truth, while she stands waiting with a new birthright in her hands which cannot be conferred until the old idols have been utterly renounced.

Leagues of sweet earth have not been devastated just to gratify a despot's pride; nor have the dead been heaped like autumn leaves merely to provide a physical expansion for the race.

Such conclusions would not only be wanton, but illogical, for the psychology of history shows that all great social upheavals have been caused by moral unrest, by dissatisfaction with the existing order of things, which, when it becomes intolerable, is swept away by a whirlwind of action whose blind fury unfortunately destroys good as well as evil in its course.

Not until we have suffered sufficiently from any folly are we content to forego its illusions, and so for centuries the race has turned to war as an antidote for its brooding ills, only subconsciously aware that it is in the spiritual force of united aim that the cleansing and healing properties of this remedy lie.

In the past, federations of interest have existed for the purpose of material gain, which represented the highest good, but slowly and with travail the race has outgrown this ideal as the goal of energy, and a new dream of mental and spiritual dominion is emerging from the throes of this cataclysmic war. It will be neither England, Germany, nor Russia, but the whole world that will demand a franchise, a period of peace in which to lay the foundations for her new scheme of existence, a scheme in which war as an integral factor of evolution will not be omitted, but only changed in character. Intellectual will supplant physical co-operation and combat, and international parliaments will adjust the balance of power. Modern warfare is termed a science, but the present crisis proves that it is only a faulty and too destructive medium of competition, and that it should be superseded, because physical combat is founded on an outgrown ideal, and, like a vampire, it now threatens the life that gave it birth!

Through a curious but just irony of evolution, Germany, with her "Kultur," or over-developed intellectual organism, has been made the scapegoat of civilization in this world struggle.

If any other country has been secretly cherishing a similar dream of individual power, it must stand drastically healed of such folly by the exhibition of madness and shame to which this illusion has goaded the self-victimized "Huns."

Their frenzied menace has shaken England out of her normal lethargy, and turned France from her skepticism. In the face of this Teuton arrogance, Russia has renounced her greed, Poland has abjured her hatred, America has learned reverence, Japan has vindicated her strength, India has overcome her prejudices, and Belgium has sacrificed her fair body.

Viewed in the light of these sacrificial flames, we cannot help regarding Germany with mingled awe and gratitude, for she presents a human oblation on the altar of time, an oblation that will enable man to take one step nearer to eternity.

The race has cast itself into the scale of destiny, and in the balance there lies one grain of wisdom!

That grain has many facets. The message of color, like that of other waiting revelations, cannot be fully made until this war has defined the limitations of form and exploded the myth of material might. That point elucidated, we shall be able to turn our attention to this new science of color, which is the rainbow revelation that will fulfil the glorious Biblical prophecy of universal peace and God's everlasting mercy to man (cf. Genesis ix, vv. 13 and 14): "I do set my bow in the cloud, and it shall be for a token of a covenant between me and the earth." "And it shall come to pass, when I bring a cloud over the earth, that the bow shall be seen in the cloud: and I will remember my covenant, which is between me and you and every living creature of all flesh."

In the following chapters I shall endeavor to show the practical relation that color bears to various activities of life, and I shall indicate methods for the application of this knowledge.

With confidence I predict that through the study of this color-science in all its branches a more highly attuned and efficient organism can and will be evolved. The race will then find itself not only able but eager to master the new problems created by an expanded vision.

For the achievement of this development, however, it is essential that there should be a cohesion of the scattered labor and love that have been individually brought to bear upon the study of color.

In Chapter IV. of this work, I have enumerated a few of the names and records of such workers, and to them, as to the many others that must exist, I send this urgent cry for a speedy co-operation.

Let them come forward and endorse my appeal for a' color college and a color theater, where the fruits of their research shall be accessible to all, and where they will find a wider field for experiment than any they have yet known. I believe that as a medium for general development and inquiry, a color theater should and will precede a color college.

For the past five years I have devoted my thought to the working possibilities of such an institution. I have also met a composer who has entered into the color thought in relation to music, and with whom I have collaborated on a score which is now complete. I have written various plays for color production. These plays are worked out in correct color groupings, designed to create the psychological interest which in the written drama has been supplied by words.

Through the dignified production of such plays the masses will become sensitized to color and in this manner be gradually prepared to acquire the various benefits that a scientific understanding of this message can confer.

Then, in due course, the color college will supply exact knowledge and training to all. Meanwhile, I claim the reader's earnest consideration and indulgence for these shadowy outlines of a vast subject, and I urge his enthusiasm and support for the foundation of a color theater and a color college. In the luminous era upon whose threshold we stand, art and science will coalesce and become aware of their profound kinship, and those of us who have been privileged in any capacity to pave the way for this march of progress will be reverently grateful for the vision of this long-promised and divine union.

CHAPTER II COLOE AS AN INDICATION OF EVOLUTION

What is color?

For some, only a matter of course; for others, an aesthetic pleasure or an interesting scientific phenomenon, the result of vibrations of light acting upon different substances and upon our optic nerves.

But there are those for whom color means more than this, because in it they find health and music; in short, the very song of life and the spiritual speech of every living thing.

Even to an indifferent observer, the color of a thing constitutes one of its chief appeals, the reason for this being that color is an unerring index of the hidden forces of that thing by which we are either attracted or repelled.

In the case of inanimate objects, we incline to favor colors that are complementary to our own color vibrations, because they have a soothing, satisfying effect, and furnish us with elements in which we are lacking.

For speaking thus prematurely of "color vibrations," I must ask indulgence, but in Chapter IV., in which the color system of the individual is diagnosed, this term is explained at length.

Meanwhile, let us consider the value of color as a general index. We may say, that in reference to living organisms, color is always a dual statement, since it indicates immediate conditions, and forecasts the next phase of evolution.

The green of spring informs us that the sap is rising in the trees; it also predicts that the gold of autumn must follow.

By its hue, we know when a flower is about to fall; and the plumage of birds and skins of beasts are renewed according to the necessity of their lives, for in the mating season they are furnished with the brilliant hues that attract, and that bespeak abundant vitality.

By color, as well as by cleavage, the history of rocks and shells is known; and color largely determines the age and nature of man.

Why, then, should he not awaken to the fact that it may and does control other issue of his destiny besides the physical one?

Abdul-Baha, the great Persian seer and the present leader of the Bahi movement, has said that we should live in our bodies as in a crystal case, through which we can see clearly on all sides; but, he pithily adds, "No one can dust the outside of this case but ourselves!"

Clarity of vision, therefore, is the result of an inner, not of an outer process, and in placing these notes of mine before you, I am only in the position of a person who holds up a lantern and discloses an avenue.

Whether that avenue is worth exploring, each one must decide for himself, and if he does consider it worth while to do so, the energy that he develops in the process of groping his own way, will also enable him "to brush the dust off" another side of his case.

I intend only to indicate this color kingdom in a general and sweeping fashion, but though the vision which I bring to bear on the subject be like a searchlight which briefly reveals a shrouded landscape, it has at least the merit of springing from direct experience.

The panoramic circumstances of my life, allied to a deep love of nature, have been the stimuli and source of my research and conclusions.

Born in India, the nomadic spirit of the Orient is strong in my veins. I have lived in England, America, Africa, China, and France successively, and I have visited Australia, Japan, Germany, Italy, and Belgium, so I can claim fairly an international area of observation.

In experiment, I have pursued my way through ridicule and many other absurdities to reach even a small clearing in the forest of doubts and difficulties that surround this complex question; and had I not been growingly convinced of the metaphysical as well as the physical benefits to be derived from a proper understanding of color, I could hardly have continued in my solitary quest. As in my case, observation was the incentive to experiment, I will, first of all, give a few deductions culled from travel notes made on the influence that color exerts upon nations, children, and animals.

This fundamental classification of correspondence is important, because when elaborated and analyzed it has a vital bearing upon the ethical, educational, and sensory values of color. Nations respond to color as plants do to the sun. They blossom and bear fruit physically, mentally, and morally in answer to the waves of color with which they are surrounded. In other words, the human inhabitants of any part of the globe are the completion of its landscape, inasmuch as they focus in themselves the potencies of the color waves that distinguish that particular bit of the earth. Thus the heart of a land is trans-muted to the soul of a people, for nations express the potencies of color with purpose, whereas nature can only do so with passion.

Here you will meet me with the objection that in a few hundred years a nation changes appreciably, while its natural surroundings remain practically unaltered. The Aegean Sea is presumably as blue today as it was a thousand years ago, but what are the modern Greeks compared to their heroic ancestors'? True, but it is the body and soul, *not* the brain of a nation, that respond to color. The brain is only the vehicle or instrument through which the potencies of color express their purpose, and when this instrument gets worn out or atrophied, the nation becomes mentally negative for some hundreds of years, and is unable to express what possibly it apprehends.

One has only to study history for a corroboration of this fact, and one finds that every period of mental efflorescence has been followed by a period of collapse, chaos, and nullity. From this mental and moral debris, new economic structures rise slowly, and furnish the necessary elevation from which the mental eye can regain vision, and take more than a utilitarian survey of its surroundings. This is the point at which a nation again becomes responsive to the color waves of its country.

For instance, it is through no mere hyperbole that China has won for herself the epithets "celestial" and "flowery." The exquisite poets of the T'ang dynasty, the profound Confucius, and the patient, heroic masses of this country are alike the reflectors, through whom the transparent azure, lavender, indigo, emerald, and rose of Chinese landscapes have been transmuted into sublime verse, and into that stoic, cleareyed philosophy which is the glory of the "Sons of Han." Indeed, one has only to stand on a Chinese hillside in April, and absorb the rainbow effect of pale-green rice fields against miles of cherry and peach bloom, delicately fringed with golden millet, to feel even in one's own superficially attuned organism a reflex of the calm and penetration that characterizes Chinese life and literature. What has happened actually is this: unconsciously we have merged with the landscape, and the life of those pure and brilliant colors has had its definite effect upon us.

Passing from the nation to the infant, we find that till they are about ten, children's color sense is either dormant or restricted to bright "mental" colors, for which youngsters of all lands have a predilection.

This fact can be accounted for by the general law that the colors preferred are usually those which are complementary to the creature's phase of development. Children, therefore, respond to the mental colors that represent the growth towards which they are straining. They become easily exhausted by color, and cannot concentrate for long on any one tint. Their expanding intelligence demands a constant change, to enable them to endure the strain of the vibrations to which they are awakening. Ask a child to choose a balloon from one of those floating pyramids of color that most of us have loved in infancy, and he will have the greatest difficulty in making a decision—he will probably want them all.

The trained mind, on the contrary, allied with a developed color sense, demands either a concentration of color or many gradations that combine in a subtle symphony of one tint. The massive but perfectly modulated brilliance of Oriental tapestries is typical of this complex color sense.

The colors which chiefly affect animals are scarlet, saffron, and grass green. Caged birds are stimulated by grass green, snakes can be hypnotized by yellow, and many birds and quadrupeds respond to both red and yellow.

My observation leads me to believe, however, that animals are sensitive to all colors in a more or less degree, and that their very decided response to a few tints is due to the fact that they hear as well as see the vibrations of color, and that saffron, green, and scarlet may owe their marked influence to tone rather than to tint. To be certain of such a theory, however, one would need considerably more proof than I have yet been able to collect.

CHAPTER III DEFINITIONS AND PURPOSES OF COLOR

Before I began consciously to study color, I was already much preoccupied with, form; indeed, my profound appreciation of sculpture was one of the channels through which I became aware of the subtler medium of expression that links us with the universal plan.

The mythological masterpieces of the ancients, and many of Auguste Rodin's symbolical groups, such as "The Hand of God" and "The Muse," seem to furnish an ironical commentary on form *per se,* even from these master craftsmen. Their works are often winged with a great weariness and a great longing, that uplift one to the realm of rapid vibrations into which they must have entered through their achievement.

Rodin's works, perhaps more than those of any other sculptor, symbolize what Fechner would have called the entity of the planet; and it is this comprehensive and luminous quality in them that, for me, has always constituted their chief appeal.

In this connection I will touch upon some theories of the scientist philosopher, as though my sensitivity to color had led me to similar conclusions long before I had the happiness of reading Fechner's works, I feel that some direct quotations from his *"ZendAvesta"* will voice the relationship of color to the universe and to this planet, with a beauty and finality that no expression of mine could achieve.

Fechner regarded the earth as a conscious entity, possessed of pulses and perceptions, an entity in whose superior organism we are mere molecules.

He stated, furthermore, that the individual's happiness and growth were dependent upon a sympathetic expansion which rendered him aware of this intimate connection with the larger life of the planet. Such ideas bear a close kinship with the thought of Egypt, Greece, and Persia, and with the writings of Plato and Aristotle. Compare the utterances of such sages with these sublimely pantheistic passages from the pen of Fechner:

"As our bodies belong to the greater and higher individual body of the earth, so our spirits belong to a greater and higher individual spirit of the earth, which comprises all the spirits of earthly creatures, very much as the earth body comprises their bodies."

And again:

"As all the stars considered materially belong to the material universe, so all the spirits of stars belong to the spirit of the universe, i. e., the Divine Spirit. At the same time their own individuality and independence is as little impaired by this circumstance as our own spirits are by their connection with the earth spirit; it is their common link, their highest conscious union."

And in another work, entitled *"On Life after Death,"* we find the following, which has an almost prophetic bearing upon the coming color era:

"Through heavenly space, the earth floats along, an enormous eye immersed in an ocean of the light which proceeds from numberless stars, and wheeling round and round to receive on all sides the impact of its waves, which cross a million of times without ever disturbing each other.

"It is with that eye, man shall one day learn to see, meeting with the spreading waves of his future life the outward waves of the surrounding ether, and undisturbed by the encountering waves, penetrating with its most subtle vibrations into the depth of heaven."

Following, figuratively, 'on the lines of Fechner's philosophy, we might classify form, color, and sound as the senses of the earth, since it is owing to contact, the contact of matter with matter, and matter with ether and electricity, that these three phenomena are due. The understanding of the earth senses, like that of our own, is but a means to an end, i. e., the evolution of the race, accomplishing itself through new mediums of expression.

Let us take the first earth sense— form— and let us note how we have availed ourselves of its benefits, and through what channels we have grown to understand it.

In the beginning we used the products of the earth for sustenance and healing; then we learned to till the soil, to sow seed, and to combine the results of our toil till they fulfilled the requirements of our evolving needs.

Stone was quarried, wood was hewn, and both were employed in the building of dwellings.

Coal and ores were extracted from the soil, and natural formations served as models in our architecture, as, for instance, in the case of the Gothic cathedral, the aisles of which were copied from the delicate fretwork formed by forest arches.

We have studied and classified the various manifestations of form under such titles as botany, zoology, medicine, mineralogy, metallurgy, archaeology, etc. Why, then, should we not learn to analyze and classify color, and to define its various potentialities, under the comprehensive term of chromatology?

The intrinsic and relative values of form have been and are being daily more specifically demonstrated, and its powers pressed into our service.

Of the practical value of color, we have hardly formulated the rudiments.

The majority regard color (if they regard it at all) merely as an aesthetic and pleasurable relief to the uniformity of life. This frame of mind is an excellent one as far as it goes, for at least it provides a startingpoint for color studies, if the individual has a sensible appreciation of the meaning of aesthetic value.

If we analyze this term, "aesthetic value," we shall find that it implies power, the primal and essential value of anything, and not an accessory and purely ornamental attribute,, as many people think.

A beautiful animal, or a lovely plant, are pleasing to us, not only on account of the sensuous enjoyment afforded by their texture and symmetry, but because those qualifications give us an assurance of their abundant vitality, and of their capacity to minister practically to our needs. Hence the perfect plant or animal gives us a sense of complete satisfaction.

Many may consider this a prosaic and incorrect analysis of aesthetic appreciation, but to those who have felt beauty profoundly, the *use* underlying all her manifestations is evident, and constitutes one of beauty's most worshipful attributes.

It is not surprising, therefore, to find that the secret of our pleasure or displeasure in certain colors lies in their practical relation to our phase of development, and in their capacity to supply the want of some unuttered but deeply-felt need of our being.

The tints that we love at fifteen, we have generally outgrown at twenty-five, though there is one note to which the individual is constant throughout his life, and that keynote represents his dominant aspirations, be they physical, mental, or spiritual.

Our color affinities reflect our mental deficiencies and foreshadow our moral achievements, for the preferred color nearly always represents some essential quality in which we are lacking, and which, if acquired, adjusts the balance of our evolution.

The individual or the nation whose color sense is atrophied is unfortunate, for this means a lack of human vitality, without which the activities of the brain often become destructive. Try to make a person apprehend anything intellectually before they have felt the necessity for the knowledge, and the result is always sterile or disastrous, because they are apt to either forget or to misapply what knowledge they acquire. Likewise the student who approaches chromatology only in the spirit of curiosity and skepticism, courts grave dangers, and is unlikely even to grasp the fundamentals of this subject.

Color is the warm heart of nature, without which her forms would lack their most illuminating appeal, and insensibly countries repel or attract us by their color schemes.

I classify color broadly under three heads, *i.e.* physical, mental, and spiritual, and this classification is elaborated with an accompanying chart in Chapter V.

Meanwhile, let us take a few exam-

ples to illustrate the theory that the chosen color represents the lacking quality.

In savage races one finds a preference for hard, brilliant, mental colors; and this fact arises from two causes, one physiological, one psychological.

The savage dwells in caves, forests, or mud-huts, and from the darkness of these conditions he seeks a natural relief in bright ornaments and blankets.

Furthermore, in his evolving being, he has a mute profound need of some mental stimulus, and this need he voices in his choice of colors.

Mental colors represent beauty to him, because they embody mental growth, which is the essential complement of his evolutionary aspirations, and the unconscious goal of his achievement.

In most Oriental races there is a love of clear, rich, physical colors, which represent physical power. And why is this? Climatically, the Oriental is handicapped. Brought to an early maturity on all planes by the solar activity to which his land is exposed, his reservoirs of physical energy are soon stimulated and drawn upon, and this fact, coupled with his natural metaphysical tendencies, is apt to produce a bodily inertia that is a menace to his efficiency as a citizen, and that calls for recuperative stimulus. This stimulus he finds in certain colors.

Northern and western races favor the ethereal blues, grays, and purples which furnish those spiritual vibrations that the stress of our material civilization renders such a luxury. These are just a few of the many instances that prove the complementary significance of color choice. The ancients, who were less impeded by the complexities of an objective civilization, and who regarded life itself as the supreme art, and the matter most worthy their consideration, were well aware of the value of color, its relation to sound and number, and its practical bearing upon individual life.

The Egyptians, Hebrews, and Chaldeans assigned a color and a number to each letter of their alphabet, and the Persian Sufis had four "Schools of Color," in which they developed their perceptions. Gold was devoted to development through the understanding of beauty, green was dedicated to piety, black to intellect and wisdom, white to ecstasy and inspiration. So, through varying ages and lands, we find man possessing a subconscious and a conscious knowledge of the value of color, and modern science is daily proving the truth of the ancient hermetic teachings.

The late Dr. Mount Bleyer, of New York, made some remarkable experiments with color and sound, the result of which has been published in pamphlet form.

In Austria and Germany, also, various psychological experiments have been made with color, and its importance as a definite factor in our evolution has been emphasized in the writings of Berliner, Mitzcherling, Schopenhauer, Bimbaud, and Bene Ghyl.

In chromoscopy, or color-healing, I understand that Mr. William Heald, of Liverpool, has made many experiments, and a certain Harley Street practitioner is "testing" the value of color as a cure for nervous complaints.

Professor Wallace Eimington, of Queen's College, has constructed a color organ, for the purpose of creating what he calls the "art of mobile color," and this instrument projects color in rhythmic sequences upon clear backgrounds that are formed by screens of linen and other materials.

The effects produced on various audiences by this exhibition prove, says Professor Eimington, that "the color sense is not only latent in all of us, but that it is highly susceptible to education."

Mr. F. "W. Fraetas, of Maitland, Cape Town, one of the most advanced and devoted workers in the color cause, is constructing instruments for the scientific application of color principles, in reference to therapeutics and education. Do the researches and experiments of these thoughtful men not lead us to the obvious conclusion that color is becoming a definite factor in our evolution, and that it contains answers to many new needs arising from an increasingly complex civilization?

I think that one of the most remark-able results of the growing pressure of existence is the creation of a new and nervous type, in whom the brain has become the enemy of the body.

Formerly the body was the enemy of the brain, and excessive physical vitality rendered such remedies as "bleeding" and "blistering" essential, whereas now we are subject to disorders that call for such ethereal antidotes as thought, nature, and color cures.

In England, America, and Germany the most advanced medical practitioners are availing themselves of such resources. May we not infer from this that, as a race, we have practically subordinated the lower physical plane, and are beginning to fight our way through the more subtle difficulties of our mental evolution?

Having gradually become aware of the limitations of form, are we not reaching out to an understanding of this formless medium of color, that second sense of nature about which we, as yet, know so little, but through whose potency, undreamed-of resonances may be awakened in the mysterious heart of this planet and in our own vibrant organism? *In this Chart the Golden Circle represents Etheri the Violet space, Earthi the White space, the Head of Mani la, 6 and c corresponding respectively to his Right, his Spiritual and his left Eyei the Spiritual Eye being situated in the center of the Forehead. 1, 2 and 3 represent respectively the Physical, Mental and Spiritual Systems with their Subdivisions of Sedative, Recuperative and Stimulant Colors.*

The Three Color Systems With Their Subdivisions 1i The Physical *Sedative*
  Lead Gray
  Prune
  Terra Cotta Moss Green
Recuperative
  Golden Brown Turquoise
Stimulant
  Vermilion 2i The Mental
Sedative
Olive Green
Recuperative
  Rose Madder
  Fawn
  Royal Blue

  Emerald Green *stimulant*
Violet
  Chrome 8; The Spiritual
Sedative
Moonlight Blue
Recuperative
  Orange
  Flame Rose *Stimulant*
Eau de Nil
  Mauve
  Citron
  Azure Blue CHAPTER IV
A COLOR CHART
Science has proved that the retina of the eye is capable, actually, of only three color sensations, *i.e.,* blue, red, and yellow, and that all other sensations are the result of combinations of these colors.

I also base my color-chart, or classification, upon these three colors, which I take as keynotes.

Blue, yellow, and red are the nodes of the individual spectrum, and the many truths of color lie within the triangle formed by these points.

Color falls into three natural divisions or systems—physical, mental, and spiritual, with subdivisions of sedative, recuperative and stimulant color, of which red, yellow, and blue are the respective keynotes.

The frontis color chart may help to elucidate this statement, though it cannot claim to be more than an approximate tabulation for general guidance. It would be impossible to give an illustration that could adequately express the subdivisions and subtleties of tint that exist, and even in this general chart the pigments that are available cannot convey any idea of the differences of texture that are an allimportant factor in determining to what class, mental, physical, or spiritual, a color belongs. It is needless to add that nicety of judgment in these points is the outcome of long study and a developed color sense.

To do justice to spiritual colors, they would have to be imbued with a tingling phosphorescent quality, which no medium that I know of could give.

Many physical colors possess a gelatinous gleam which it is impossible to reproduce, and most mental colors have a crystalline transparency; therefore, in studying my limited color chart, the reader must exercise his imagination considerably if he would gather any idea of the range that it is designed to suggest.

In my chart I tabulate color broadly in three systems of seven rays each. Of the subdivisions existing between each color, it is impracticable to make a standard estimate, as they necessarily vary in number according to a person's degree of development.

Where one man recognizes only three or four gradations of tone between each color, another man is conscious of twenty or thirty.

My chart, nevertheless, is not altogether an arbitrary one, for I have constructed it from the result of experiments made on others as well as on myself, and also from the color data amassed during my travels in different lands.

The development of the color sense in the majority is unfortunately so mediocre that for the present any finality in the composition of a color chart is not possible, and I only offer the result of my research as an approximate guide.

One interesting fact that my experiments have established with some certainty, is that each eye has an individual appreciation of color, the left eye as a rule preferring physical, the right eye mental colors. This general axiom bears an interesting correspondence to the occult statement of the ancients,, namely, that the right and left sides of man represent, respectively, the positive and negative forces of his being, the creative and the receptive. Spiritual colors being really intensities of vibration, or what might be termed super colors, rather than definite tones, are more often seen with the eyes shut than open.

By most people they are discerned as a diffused sensation, rather than as an actual vision.

Have you never entered an unknown room and had a vivid impression of a certain color, then, to your surprise, found on closer inspection, that actually there was not a single article of that color in the room? In such a case, the impression that you received was one of the spiritual color which pervaded that room and was apprehended by you before you responded to the other color waves of your surroundings. For, with logical precision, the individual responds first to those colors with which his own development is concerned, and if you are keyed to receive spiritual colors, they will reach you more quickly than others.

Man is in reality a stellar organism, delicately balanced between revolving realms. With his feet planted on earth, his head poised in air, he is a receiver for both material and ethereal vibrations. In the chart which illustrates this chapter, the underlying purple represents the earth; the golden circle; ether; the central triangle, with subdivisions, a universal color system as communicated to man through sensory nodes, marked *la, lb, 1c.* Since the cognition of spiritual colors is not, strictly speaking, a matter of ocular vision, I indicate it on the chart as *lb,* a point in the center of the forehead; the mental color system as *la,* focused in the right eye, and the physical color system as *1c,* corresponding to the left eye. By this sensory disposition, based upon simple observations, we find that the individual is susceptible to three distinct color circulations, which are connected with one another.

Of these connections, the colorphile gradually becomes aware, and, while fusing his entire color system into a balanced unity, he yet retains the power to use the transition points of his color circulation, either as bridges or barriers, according to his need; for he avails himself of color as others do of breath—for various purposes.

From this chart you will observe that the geometric expression of our color circulation, or color body—if I may be permitted to use such a term—is contained in three triangles.

The triangle was the ancient's symbol for truth, and the sum of the sides of three triangles is the number nine, which they regarded as symbolizing the perfection of terrestrial manifestation, the number ten representing deity.

I do not wish to force these facts upon the reader in support of the arrangement of my color chart, for exoterically it is independent of them, but to those who are interested in occult correspondence, these points will be significant.

The understanding and development of these three color systems will be an allimportant study in the future of chromatology, for they will form the instruments through which we shall voice new expressions, and augment our mental and moral resources to a point at which we shall obtain a wider freedom.

The rapidly increasing methods of immaterial communication reasonably support a supposition that we stand at the inception of a telepathic era in the history of the race.

Already we have established wireless telegraphy, wireless telephone, telepathy, thought, and color healing; it is, therefore, not irrational to believe that in time we will add color communication to this list.

Possibly aviation will be one of the chief stimuli to this branch of chromatology, for with the increase of aerial transit, vocal speech will become inconvenient, if not impossible. We shall then exchange thought by means of color codes, which we will flash to one another. Aerial conditions having reacted upon our whole organism, we shall be more highly attuned, more etheric, and we shall be able to regulate the radiations of our color systems as we now regulate our breath and choose our words.

Finally, all people will be able to see as well as to project these colored rays of speech.

We shall radiate color, as a flower exhales perfume, and through this mobile color language we shall hold a truly illumined intercourse! The race will then possess an auric Esperanto, which will perhaps prove to be the universal tongue which the world is now seeking amid a babel of converging civilizations and creeds.

To many people, such ideas as these will appear chimerical, and yet why should they, if the history of evolution is to be held of any account?

Could gesticulation have conveyed the notion of language and literature to the prehistoric man, he would probably have greeted the proposition with a grunt and an incredulous stare, yet both these things have slowly evolved with the upward progress of mankind, and he has fashioned and used them to meet his needs.

CHAPTER V THE RELATION BETWEEN COLOR AND BREATH

Having defined the three color systems, let us examine their intrinsic and their relative values to each other and to the individual.

First of all, we must grasp two important facts, namely, that whether we are conscious of it or not, color has always some effect on us; secondly, that the science of color is intimately connected with the science of breath.

Color has always one of three effects upon us—sedative, recuperative, or stimulant.

A color is sedative when it has power to induce contemplation, reflection, indifference, resignation, inception, coagulation, melancholy. It is recuperative when it can create conditions of change, balance, expansion, generosity, contentment, conception, cohesion. And stimulant colors are those which can excite hope, ecstasy, desire, aspiration, ambition, action, or which can cause liberation of thought and emotion through achievement, dispersion, joy, peace, spiritual renewal and fresh growth.

The chart of the preceding chapter indicates the disposition of these various gradations of color in the individual, and from its arrangement the reader will observe that sedatives dominate the physical, recuperatives the mental, and stimulants the spiritual color systems. For further study I now annex another tabulation which not only marks the correspondence that exists between color and breath, but shows also the harmonious balance that is preserved by the interaction of the three systems, each one of which is determined by its preponderating colors. If the student analyzes this tabulation, he will find that, ethically, its law is consonant with the larger law of evolution, whose purpose is the domination of the body to the end that the mind may be developed, the development of the mind serving in its turn as an impetus for the quickening of the spiritual or super-man.

Once he has grasped the law that relates color with breath, the chromatologist should construct his own color chart, then harmonize its three systems through an understanding of their interaction, and finally relate his individual chart with the great charts of nature and humanity.

Subtle, indeed, is the balance that can be created in our organism by this color development; but it is a delicate and gradual process fraught with danger as well as with promise.

We can err just as easily through an excessive use of spiritual stimulant colors as through a preference for physical sedatives or recuperatives.

It is for this reason, and owing to the natural instinct for self-preservation, that mental colors are generally preferred and used by the majority, as they constitute a safe middle path, between the mysteries of the senses and of the soul.

Indeed, I am certain that eight out of ten casual observers, on looking at my chart, would select the mental colors as being those most sympathetic to them.

Let us further consider the relation that exists between the color and breath systems.

Perhaps I can best explain the matter by a few simple illustrations, though to the person whose color sense is dormant, or atrophied, my examples will be somewhat obscure.

Have you ever noticed that certain colors make you draw a deep breath, you feel that you must drink in that color, and you are even inclined to hold your breath as you look at it? These are the sedative colors.

Other colors, the mental recuperatives, evoke exclamations from you, and again there are certain tints before which your eyes involuntarily close and you remain speechless because you feel drawn out of yourself by that color. These are the stimulants.

Let us amplify these illustrations by a few simple examples drawn from universal experience.

What were your sensations and actions when, after a long sojourn amid the drab tones of a city, you were suddenly confronted with the green or purple of a summer sea? Did you not drink in that color and feel suffused with it before you spoke? That green was a physical sedative that soothed your fretted nerves and gave you fresh life.

Parenthetically, I may say that it is this change of color, as much as the change of air, which works wonders for the invalid, and, in the future, color doctors will lay much stress upon this point.

On another occasion, perhaps, when your friend showed you some glowing porcelain or embroidery in which man's skill had embodied the passion of his brain, did those mental colors not evoke expressions of admiration from you, expressions which caused your breath to come and go in short, sharp vibrations?

And if you have been a wanderer over this beautiful earth, have moonlit seas or tropical dawns not caused your lids to droop? Before their intensities of light did your eyes not close, and did you not remain speechless, but liberated and floating in an immensity of color whose exact tint you would have been puzzled to define?

Eecollect and analyze your impressions under such situations, and if even one of these experiences has been yours, it will demonstrate to you the relation that exists between color and breath, and from this simple proof you can draw your own complex deductions.

It is important that each one should endeavor to create his own color chart, for its determination is so subtle and intimate a matter that it is better, if possible, to rely on one's own judgment for its construction.

The delays and difficulties caused by one's own mistakes are more beneficial and productive than those which might be incurred through the mistakes of another.

If my chart is sympathetic to you, by all means adopt it and work with it, but remember that the confidence in a teacher must be absolute before their guidance can yield good results.

So, again I say, it is wiser to seek for yourself and slowly find than to follow hastily and fearfully in the footprints of another.

I should always prefer to assist a student to discover his own chart, rather than work it out for him.

But, you will ask, how can this workingout be accomplished?

Whether you are insensitive to color, or whether you only require to stimulate your color sense, the first step that you must take is to meditate on color in nature, and to note and tabulate the results of your work.

In any land, sky, or sea-scape, you can find large pools of color, in which you must immerse your consciousness.

During this process of concentration remain quiescent, let thought and deduction come after, but for the moment just focus your attention on the color whose vibrations you desire to understand, holding yourself mentally and physically in as negative and relaxed a condition as possible.

At first your experiment may yield no response, but is any alphabet learned in one day?

If you have the patience to practice with care ten or fifteen minutes daily, at the end of a week you may be astonished at your progress.

From my chart you can select any color with whose potencies you are in sympathy, and, finding the reproduction of that color in nature, you can test it in the crucible of your own consciousness, and discover if it has the same message for you as it has had for me.

If it has, accept my definition of it: it not, label it as you have found it yourself, whether sedative, recuperative, or stimulant. In this manner you can gradually build up your chart.

The colors of nature have a vitality not possessed by artificial colors, and therefore it is better to work with them; but if temperamentally you are handicapped by indifference, or an aversion to nature, then this experiment would probably fail, and you must employ some other means of developing your color sense.

There are many methods, but the nature one is the healthiest and safest, and it can be used with advantage by skeptic and sensitive alike.

If you experiment along these lines, you will discover to which colors you are most responsive, and you can either increase your sympathy with their potencies, or you can develop your sympathy with colors which have hitherto had no particular message for you.

This, however, is a secondary step, and the first task for the student of chromatology is to assure himself by practical experiment of the potentiality of color, of its relation to breath, and of its influence upon his own organism.

Having once done this, he can begin to construct his color chart, or to verify mine.

This undertaking he will find no mere child's play, but a very real labor.

Like all other foundations, those of chromatology must be carefully laid, otherwise the superstructures will be unstable and unsatisfactory.

Therefore it is poor economy to stint time and energy on this initial step, and if you once realize the practical as well as the ethical advantage to be derived from an understanding of color, you will not object to making a gradual progress.

No profound or vital question can be answered off-hand, and if it is worth while to ask yourself this question at all, it is worth while to extract from yourself a reliable and stimulating answer.

I have practically devoted my life to acquiring what I consider mere rudiments of this vast subject, but even these rudiments have enlarged and illumined existence for myself and for others, and it is with the object of placing certain tested benefits of color within the reach of all that this little book is written.

My thought is only one of the heralds who, with increasing insistence, are proclaiming the existence of this kingdom of subtler emotions, profounder ideas, and more quickened spiritual perceptions. Not only art, but science herself, the great initiate of truth, is daily bringing her lens to bear upon this problem.

Having discussed the effect of color upon the individual, let us now consider the relation of the individual to color.

Of the lay reader, I must request an effort of imagination, for he must try and realize that he himself is actually a living battery of mobile color, and that, like the sun, he rays forth, shines, or is obscured according to his condition and development; in short, he is the sum-total of his threecolor systems.

Already these radiations of color are perceptible to some of us, and as the organism of the whole race evolves to a higher rate of vibration, they will become visible to all.

If you ray forth, or project your own color vibrations with sufficient intensity, you can amalgamate them with nature's universal reservoirs, participating in their life, and thereby augmenting your own vitality.

If you only shine, or project color in a limited degree, you only enjoy a limited vitality, and, if you are obscured, *i.e.,* unable or unwilling to radiate color, you are either most unhappy, or leading a negative, mechanical existence that is a disgrace to any living thing. From these statements it is obvious that the condition or power of raying forth is the most desirable one.

But how can one attain to this condition, and what does it imply?

It implies that we are expressing ourselves adequately, consequently that we are happy, and that we are spreading happiness around us.

This state is achieved unconsciously, when we find ourselves in a sympathetic color environment (whether we are aware of the color or not), but *it can be achieved at will, anywhere, if we understand the interaction of our three color systems, and their relation to our environment.*

If certain colors can induce certain states, is it not reasonable to suppose that certain states can induce certain colors!

Yes. The tones of your voice, and the trend of your thoughts and feelings create waves of color in which you move, encircled as in an aureole, and through which you react upon the atmosphere and upon people around you.

If, then, we find ourselves in an alien atmosphere, we must either succumb to or dominate it, as we judge most advisable, and we can only consciously do either of these things through an exact knowledge of the interaction of our three color systems, and their relation to the general atmosphere at any given moment.

We find, therefore, that the inner and outer color charts are indissolubly allied, namely, that our individual color system has a definite relation to our environment.

We discover our own chart most truly and profoundly by studying that of nature and of our fellow-men, and again the significance of these universal charts is more fully revealed as our own color sense develops.

In reality, therefore, there is only one great color chart, *i.e.,* the color chart of the planet, and, like a half discovered and alluring kingdom, it is emerging slowly from the mists of manifestation, luminous with promise of the new powers and sensibilities of which our evolution stands in need.

Happily there are many pilgrims hastening towards this appearing land, and the searchlights of science are circling round its obscurities.

CHAPTER VI HOW TO DEVELOP THE COLOR SENSE

The relation between color and breath having been indicated in the previous chapter, I may now permit myself the statement that color can be inhaled and exhaled.

Indeed, it is the vital and suble counterpart of breath, with which it is indissolubly allied, for we, no less than other molecular organisms, reflect color in response to the breath of God, or the vibrations of ether, whichever way one chooses to state the fact. But, in addition to this receptive capacity which we possess in common with the vegetable, animal, and mineral kingdoms, man transcends these kingdoms because he possesses a vibratory power which enables him to project as well as to reflect color,

and it is this creative gift that brings alike a responsibility and a freedom that is not shared by lower organisms. Man can and does react upon the atmosphere through his color system.

I am now going to outline a few preliminary methods which the student will find helpful. When you have constructed your own chart, or understood mine, in order to further develop your color sense, select whichever colors you are most in need of at the time, and work with them in the following manner.

Surround yourself actually with the color whose potency you desire, or, if this is impossible, surround yourself mentally with it. By the careful study of your chart, you will know exactly which sedative, recuperative, or stimulant you are in need of.

The method of mental color envelopment is best achieved by inducing in yourself the conditions that correspond to the color of your choice.

This is a more difficult but a surer method of development than the external use of color, though progress is certainly aided by suitable environment, and if you can employ both methods simultaneously it is an advantage.

That contemptuous phrase, '' He takes on the color of his surroundings," has more truth in it than we are aware of.

The color sensitive, liable to be too easily elated and depressed, is often the object of undeserved scorn from his more apathetic brother who remains complacent in all surroundings, but if the sensitive could only add knowledge to the feeling, he would soon confound his less developed brother.

The chromatologist of the future will command color consciously, and not be at its mercy as often for ill as for good.

Meanwhile, to those who intend to pave their own way into the color kingdom, I would say, work first with the physical sedatives, *i. e.,* gray, puce, green, or brown; then use the mental recuperatives, crimson lake, fawn, blue; advancing gradually to night blue, the spiritual sedative.

From that revert to the physical recuperatives, turquoise and russet, follow-

ing them with mental sedatives, and finally concentrate on the spiritual stimulants and recuperatives, but always work with these in pairs, *i. e.,* azure and flame-rose, or orange and mauve, etc., because the vibratory action of spiritual colors is apt to be too violent, and they have often an unbalancing effect unless used in combinations.

I annex a tabular schedule which may be useful, and if the student gives this system a fair trial, it will yield surprising results. It will gradually harmonize his three color systems, and it will assist him to a practical understanding of their interaction.

This technique, pursued along the simple lines of concentration, is a safe one, but until he has obtained considerable results with other colors, let the student work with spiritual color sparingly, and always in twos.

At the outset, no color or colors should be worked with less or more than seven consecutive days at a time, and the average study or concentration should not exceed one hour daily, divided into halves or even quarters.

For example, a month's work would be regulated in the following manner:—

First week.. Gray—physical sedative.
Second".. Crimson lake—mental recuperative.
Third week.. Night blue—spiritual sedative.
Fourth".. Chrome—mental stimulant. And these same colors should be worked with until the student has become sensitive to their message. To rush on prematurely to fresh combinations is merely to court confusion, whereas a patient trial of this rotary system of development is both sure and satisfying, and for the beginner I recommend it, in conjunction with nature study, above every other method.

Study Fob Color Development (1) *Physical Sedatives.* — Gray, puce, green, or brown.
(2) *Mental Recuperatives.*—Crimson lake, royal blue, fawn. (3) *Spiritual Sedative.*—Night blue. (4) *Mental Stimulants.*—Violet or chrome. (5) *Physical Recuperatives.* — Turquoise, russet. (6) *Mental Sedative.*—Olive green. (7)

Spiritual Stimulants and Recuperatives. —Eau de nil and flame-rose, orange, and mauve, etc.

It is true that symbols, sound, and perfume being interchangeable with color, can also be used as mediums of color development. Sound and perfume, however, must be most carefully handled, as they are almost too sensuous to give reliable results, and it is very easy to be carried away by them into harmful color excesses.

The aim of the chromatologist is to understand color as well as to feel it, and this he can do more satisfactorily through a mental than through an emotional process. Also the functioning of two senses at a time means a loss of concentration, and if you commence to study color through the medium of sound, the enjoyment that you have in sound lessens your appreciation of color. Whereas, if you are content to study color, *per se,* its synthetic life, of symbol, sound, and perfume, will gradually become revealed to you.

For beginners in chromatology, the best method of development, therefore, is through a concentration on nature's colors.

The understanding and control of sedatives and recuperatives is most helpful for the average life and the average individual, because such colors can be of practical service, and the practical advantage is the one which appeals most generally and is most generally needful.

To the modern mind, urged as it by the stress of civilization and the necessity of possessing an abundance of useful wares for exchange in the market-place, the value of color as an agent in spiritual evolution may seem of minor importance; but the ancients, who realized the practical value of spiritual growth, laid much stress upon this function of color.

Nearly all Eastern races have recognized the potencies of color. The Egyptians, Hebrews, Chaldeans, and Persians made a special study of the subject, and, as I have already mentioned, the Sufis, those mystic poet-philosophers of the tenth century, even went so far as to have "schools of color," in which the student was trained for different and definite purposes, according to the aim of his unfoldment.

If we analyze the attitude of the savage towards color, we find that he, too, regards it from a profound and devotional standpoint.

Indian and African "chiefs" paint themselves for their war dances, which have a religious significance, and many, of their bead necklets and girdles are cherished love letters.

This is the case among Zulu tribes. For, according to the arrangement of azure, amber, and scarlet beads, the recipient can measure the degree of love that the necklet or girdle professes!

CHAPTER VII THE THERAPEUTIC VALUE OF COLOR

One of the most practical branches of chromatology is color healing.

In my first chapter I touched upon this, and called attention to the fact that science. is daily probing deeper into the capacities of color as a healing agent.

The "violet rays" have long been an established cure for various complaints, and though I have no knowledge of the principles of chromoscopy, I have made personal experiments that have left me without a doubt as to the possibility of color cures.

Such cures are, however, hard to effect upon people whose color sense is undeveloped or highly developed.

In the former case, they are like an instrument that has scarcely been played on, and from which it is difficult to draw a response; and in the latter case, the color vibrations of the patient, being strong and active, are liable to interfere with one's work.

It is a difficult matter for the operator to nullify habitual and vivid color vibrations, which are often half the cause of the trouble, and these have sometimes to be counteracted before a curative current can be established.

Double work is thus entailed.

It may happen that environment is another obstacle that has to be overcome, but if the patient and environment cooperate with the healer, his task is not a hard one.

Generally speaking, men seem to be more susceptible to color than women, and the most responsive patient is the average individual who appreciates color, and is not hampered with violent prejudices for or against.

I have not, so far, practiced color healing professionally or even extensively, but the result of my experiments have been sufficient to convince me of the power of my medium, and of the importance of this branch of chromatology.

Color cures are especially adapted to nervous and blood troubles, because through the breath system color acts directly upon the blood system, and therefore indirectly upon the nervous system, though a few nervous centers are directly responsive to color.

When one remembers that color indicates the nature of a thing, and that color is contained in all the vegetable and mineral ingredients of drugs, does color healing seem such an unreasonable hypothesis?

Medicine has combined and transmuted the solids of nature into various compounds for the benefit of man.

Why should another science not arise which will combine and transmute the more ethereal emanations of nature to meet the requirements of our rapidly etherealizing organism?

I have found that greens, reds, and yellows have the most powerful healing properties, and with combinations of these colors I have obtained some striking results.

In one case the eyesight of a young writer was restored. He was threatened with blindness, and suffered with nervous headaches.

I have alleviated both insomnia and dipsomania, and in one instance I was able to restore vigor to a shriveled arm, and to renew the action of a broken knee, through the scientific application of color principles.

I quote these cases more as an incentive to the student of chromatology than as any certificate for myself. Also, to many people, the power of healing bodily ills seems an all-important attribute, indeed the only one which can claim respect for a new revelation, and therefore

I wish to state definitely that this power *is* latent in color.

My own humble gropings toward the truth of this vast subject only merit consideration in so far as they are sincere, and have, in a small measure, been productive of good.

I am well aware, however, that color healing cannot be called anything but empirical, until it is based upon a mass of statistics collected from scientific observations, and condensed into scientific formulae. It is ardently to be hoped that color will merit this official recognition from skilled men of science at no distant date, and that those who are already preoccupied with this subject will give more publicity to the results of their research.

Personally, I believe that the chromatophilist, or certificated color doctor, is by no means so remote a possibility.

The color wave has rolled far on its way from the horizon of truth; it is gathering power in its progress, it is sweeping more and more thinkers into its vortex, and when it breaks in fullness upon the shores of humanity, this little book will only be one of the many heralds that shall have proclaimed its coming.

CHAPTER VIII THE COLOR DEVELOPMENT OF THIRTEEN COUNTRIES

Color preference, as I have shown, is in some degree an index of character, for people usually incline to the colors that are complementary to their own color vibrations, because the former supply them with vibrations in which they are lacking. I have made some notes of interest in this connection upon the color preference of various countries that I have visited.

Generally speaking, the older the culture of a country, the finer is its color sense and the more complex its color expression.

I place India, China, Northern Africa, and Persia first, followed in order of merit by Egypt, Japan, Italy, Holland, France, America, England, Germany, and Australia.

China and Persia are the true aristocrats in this matter, as much on account of their choice as of their subtle craft in handling color.

In no other countries that I know of can one find such a use and understanding of azure, indigo, vermilion, electric mauve, and citron yellow, which constitute the scale of spiritual stimulants that dominate the color expression of these lands.

Not only in woven, lacquered, or painted masterpieces, but also in the ordinary implements of life, one finds these exquisite vibrations repeated.

Even the wearing apparel of the Chinese is remarkable for its delicate brilliance.

A Chinese interior may be sombre and stately, but it forms a perfect setting for its inhabitants.

Clad in exotic splendor that belies the ivory indifference of their faces, the slim "celestials" are well framed in their blackwood and ebony chairs.

The tranquillity of the atmosphere (for except during typhoons there is seldom storm or wind), as well as their rainbowtinted landscape, is largely responsible for the aesthetic and intellectual development that has always characterized the Chinese.

It is a significant fact that in this country the scholars rank in importance with princes and statesmen. Whenever the late Empress Dowager Tzu-Hsi indulged in some flagrant breach of "precedent," one of her first anxieties was to propitiate the "literati," by issuing verbose manifestos in which her crafty flattery of their political importance as a power in the State regained her a measure of their support.

We find, therefore, that the Chinese, being pre-eminently a mental race, incline in their color expression to spiritual stimulants.

In Persia atmospheric conditions, resembling to a great extent those of China, have tended rather to mystic and emotional growth, and the color expression here inclines to mental recuperatives and stimulants.

This trend is also reflected in Persian literature, and any student of Hafiz, Rumi, or Omar must have been struck by the abundant use of color in their works, suggested as well as expressed.

The Hindus, the Arabs, and the tribesfolk bordering the northern coast of Africa (the latter descended from Egyptians, Carthagenians, and Phoenicians), are essentially mystic peoples, therefore in India and Africa we find that mental and physical recuperatives predominate.

Scarlet, turquoise, cobalt, crimson lake, purple, umber, terra-cotta, and greens form the basis of their color schemes.

In India and Africa, also, the great snows and the great deserts, so prismatic in their whiteness, are largely responsible for a physical inertia that the inhabitants of these countries unconsciously seek to alleviate by their color preferences.

The dazzling vistas of sunlit snow and sand are over-stimulating to their color sense, and in their continuous environment danger lurks, for they develop mental and spiritual, in excess of physical vibrations, and consequently are apt to engender a physical languor that menaces the material well-being of a race.

In Egypt, Japan, and Italy the color sense is vital and distinguished by peculiarities.

Egypt is allied to India in color expression, though more limited.

There is the same use of recuperatives, and we find a predominance of turquoise, scarlet, terra-cotta, and black, the abundant use of the last-named being very significant.

The spiritual colors, however, were, and are, seldom, if ever, used by this hermetic and intellectual race.

Japan presents the phenomenon of a country that has evolved a kind of phantom color chart, composed of ghostly colors, that are difficult to define.

The Japanese grays, lavenders, browns, yellows, purples, and greens are such etherealized editions of physical and mental sedatives and recuperatives that they form almost a new scale of stimulants. This scale, though lacking in intensity, has the charm of a very subtle balance; in fact, it possesses the effect of an incense in which the ingredients are so suavely mingled that one cannot differentiate them.

Orange and a peculiar vivid pink are the only spiritual stimulants employed by the Japanese, and these are used sparingly.

Their handling of black, the negative color factor, is remarkable. So dextrously is it used, in their decorative art that through its juxtaposition sedatives are often artificially rarefied to a degree approaching recuperatives, and mental colors etherealized almost to spiritual stimulants, and sometimes even suggested in spaces where they do not actually exist.

This color impressionism is as evident in Japanese literature as it is in their other national expressions, in their music, and in their clothing.

Theirs is an eminently practical genius. Gifted as a race with an overflowing vitality, they have had to express themselves within the limits of a small country, and this has given all their output an essential quality. They have cultivated discrimination, which has resulted in an aesthetic taste that is unique.

From the surface of many things they create one product, and like their dwarf trees, their condensed color chart, though not altogether satisfactory, is remarkably interesting and effective. Too intermingled to be profound, it has, nevertheless, an original appeal possessing value and purpose. It is an affirmative glorification of negative virtues!

Possibly my first impressions of Japan may serve as an illustration of this paradox, and may therefore be considered a pardonable digression.

I had always dreamed of the Mikado's country as a land of dazzling pagodas, and kimonos, brilliant as butterflies. On my arrival there one March day, I was amazed to find "Nippon" emerging silver and brown from opalescent sea mists. The fragile houses built of shaded woods closely resembled those large brown moths with silvery under-wings.

It was a pearl gray morning, and light snow showers mingled with the drifting plum-bloom.

This first ethereal effect repeated itself constantly, for whether watching the stream of gray and brown kimonos meandering through pink cherry orchards, or when enjoying the beauty of black-and-white lanterns swaying in the lavender dusk, the color expression of Japan always seemed a phantom creation, born of the fading twilight, and tinged with the glow of dawn, in just such an impalpable degree as dew that is tinged with the prism.

On the most brilliant summer day, a Japanese landscape retains this liquid and evanescent quality, a fact due to the rapidly changing atmospheric pressures, and probably also this is one of the causes of the synthetic color development of the people. In Japan, color waves follow each other with such rapidity that the life of one is barely perceived before another begins to make itself felt, and the Japanese skim, as it were, the surface of each wave, and condense the result of its reaction into their phenomenal color expression.

In Italy I was disappointed. The vulgarity of modern Italian color expression might lead one to suppose that the Latin color sense was focused in those great painters whose names have immortalized this land, or possibly that Italy is undergoing a period of transition. I incline to this latter conclusion, because, though vulgar, the Italian color sense is exceedingly vital, and its expression exuberant. Mental and physical colors are massed together indiscriminately, and sometimes in distressing discords. If a house is painted outside and inside, it is painted all over with meaningless and intricate designs, and this diffuse ornamentation spoils even the interior of many stately galleries. But for centuries the Latin race has been preoccupied with form, to the exclusion of other aesthetic perceptions, and this may account for what would otherwise be a phenomenon in a sensitive, artistic people.

Perhaps Futurism, that dynamic revolution, which represents the aesthetic soul of young Italy (vociferating still harshly in its new language), may yet proclaim color development as one of its final issues.

The Futurists have created a new scale and a new treatment of color in pictorial art, a scale of physical stimulants that are as tingling with vitality as are the poems of Filippo Marinetti, the gifted founder of the movement. From this seismic condition Italy may yet emerge as one of the leaders of color science.

The remaining sextet of countries, I will dismiss, with cursory comments, as their color expression shows no marked individuality.

In Holland and America, the color development is vital; in France it is complex, though somewhat degenerate; in England, rather atrophied, but daily stirring to new life.

Of all western lands that I have visited, Germany is the least advanced. This fact is significant of her lack of human development, and of her bulbous mental "Kultur."

The Teuton color sense is coarse, and runs to extremes of neutrality and garishness. What could be more distressing than the modern German movement in decorative art?

Its crude pretensions are mere immaturity masquerading as originality.

I understand that this gaudy manifestation is an off-shoot of the perversion which was known as New Art, and it is to be hoped that it may die the same ignominious death.

It is hard to believe that a country which has produced such great musicians should be so insensible to color. And yet, this is perhaps one of the solutions of the problem, for whereas in the past the Latin has expressed color through form, the Teuton has unconsciously expressed it through sound. Yet it is a sad comment upon existing conditions in Germany that Strauss, the foremost among modern German composers, has in his biggest works, degraded a great genius to the same garish dissonance and decadence that distinguishes German color expression. The operas of Strauss are pandemoniums of musical dissolution, through which divine harmonies float like fallen angels mourning for their lost estate.

Now, however, that color is becoming an essential medium of expression for all races, both Germany and Italy are responding to its call. Italy through the aesthetic movement of Futurism, and Germany through scientific research, and by these devious paths both countries will achieve their salvation in due course.

Of Australia, I can only say that it has just emerged from the "bush"! Like an astonished child, it is slowly rubbing its eyes open, and I doubt if it knows yet whether the "wattle" is green or gold. But the color wave is sweeping all shores in its approach, and Australia, no less than Germany and Italy, will benefit by this tidal onrush.

CHAPTER IX THE EDUCATIONAL IMPORTANCE OF COLOR

Having dealt with the nature of the color sense, let us examine the causes of its development and atrophy, and let us consider in what ways it would be possible at this preliminary stage of the new science to include color study in educational curriculums. For though the color theater is essential as a general educator, much could be achieved in elementary training which would prepare graduates for the color college of the future.

We have seen that the color sense of nations varies, and that the degree of color development and the nature of color expression are dependent upon the character of the color sense.

If this is fine and discriminating, the two resultants are fine and extensive; if coarse, they are crude and limited.

Also the fundamental influence of natural environment must be borne in mind as the chief determining factor in the nature of these things.

But in the evolution of a perception, as of everything else, growth is registered by rhythmic phases. So we find the color sense waxing and waning in the same country.

For instance, in the fifteenth century Italy produced masterpieces of color in painting and brocades; and the pageant of her civil life was a festival in itself.

That she has now degenerated into color mediocrity is a deplorable fact, and yet we find her need of renaissance crying aloud through the Futurist movement.

In the individual, color sense and expression, at a first glance, often seem independent of the influence of environment; but this is rarely so, for if you examine such a case, you will probably find that the person in question has been obliged to live in distasteful surroundings, and has consequently created a mental color environment which has been the actual initiative of his color sense.

This is the painful experience of many sensitives who find themselves born into countries and families that are alien to them.

The consequence is that the antipathy produced by their actual surroundings causes them to turn for comfort to a mental world of their own creation, where, if only for a time, they can be free and at rest.

The emotions induced by these thought environments generate a reflex vibratory action in the individual, that creates around him color waves in which he expands and finds a self-expression that is denied him in the ordinary conditions of his life.

Through repetition, these color waves form a creative background, which is the real source of that man's color sense and development. Generally speaking, therefore, individual and national color development are dependent on the same laws, and, though apparently stimulated by external conditions, they are in reality regulated by profound psychological necessities.

The atrophy of the color sense, like its development, is usually due to so-called external conditions.

But at the outset of this book we postulated agreement with the scientist philosopher Fechner, who regarded the planet as a living entity in whose organism we are but molecules. Following this train of thought, we defined color as the second sense of the earth, and if we adhere to this pantheistic symbolism, we cannot consider any phenomenon as "external" in the accepted sense of that word. Comparative study shows that color atrophy is regulated largely by the same causes as color development, and if we take England as an example, we find that in the last four hundred years the growth of her industrial life, combined with the appearance of railroads, and smoking factories, has had an effect upon landscapes and atmosphere that has reacted badly upon the nation.

In the Elizabethan era, when agricultural activity was more important than now, and when forests and, even in towns, trees were more abundant, the color sense of the English was vital, and this vitality reflected itself in the literature and in the beautiful wearing apparel of that epoch. Many may call the moral civilization of those days into question, but I am disinclined to believe that ruffles were whiter than reputations then, and it is certain that glowing textures were worn, and that the ordinary spectacle of life was a pageant in comparison to the drab uniformity that characterizes our present crowds.

Fortunately, with the increasing use of electricity as a motor power, England is emerging from her smoky torpor, and is preparing to regain her epithet of "Merrie."

Within the last five years there has been a decided color renaissance, which has found its chief expression in woman's clothing and in decorative art.

In painting, the new life has manifested itself in violent and revolutionary movements, most of them, it is true, imported from France, such as post-impressionism, cubism, synchronism, etc., but in house decoration England shows a discretion and progress ahead of either Germany or France. In this connection it is interesting to note how countries develop diversely on contemplative and executive lines, and though Germany has probably made more scientific and pathological inquiries into color than any other nation, the result of her research seems to be pitifully sterile. On the other hand, England, though only subconsciously aware of this great color force, demonstrates its power in her daily life and surroundings, a fact that leads one to hope that she will be among the foremost to welcome chromatology in all its branches.

The English pride themselves on being a practical race, and as history records that color expression coincides with a country's periods of prosperity, why should England not hail her color renaissance with increasing attention?

A flower is at its glory when it is in full bloom, and a land is approaching one of its golden ages when the expression of its outer life reflects the glow of its inner needs and ideals.

A rose may nod its green, unbroken bud at us, and say, "I am red, soft, and fragrant," but unless it unfolds, how shall we know whether these things be true?

If color development means an increase of power in the individual and in the race— and when I say power, I mean a capacity for fuller expression on every plane,—would it not be well if chromatology were to become an essential study for all?

This thought brings us to the consideration of the necessity for color study in kindergartens and State schools. The proposition is a large and revolutionary one, and it demands a separate and detailed treatment. Meanwhile, suffice it to say that such studies could only be determined by experimental inquiry.

The color sense of the child would be *tested* before the lines of his color development could or would be decided on; but the expert professor of the future will be able to classify the training needful under one of the three following heads: physical, mental, or spiritual color development, according to the needs of the case. I am certain that this etheric tuning of the organism in childhood will prove of incalculable benefit, and will result in an increase of capacity and activity that only time and tests can verify.

The importance of this kindergarten color training will be great, because through it, the coming generation will be equipped to graduate eventually in the color college, and to grapple with the larger, subtler problems that the unfolding of this great revelation will undoubtedly present.

I am myself evolving a system of kindergarten color training, but that will be the subject of a later volume.

Meanwhile, I beg the reader's indulgence for a cursory treatment of the question, since the aims of this book must be restricted to an appeal for a universal and scientific interest in color, and an urgent plea for the foundation of a color theater, which will act as a medium towards the accomplishment of that end.

If the understanding of color can yield us bodily healing, mental control, and a subtler range of emotions and interests, surely the sooner we set about it the better. But until the color theater *is* an accomplished fact, I may say to one and all, if your color sense is atrophied or dormant owing to disadvantage of environment, seek some antidote against these limiting conditions.

Stimulate your color sense into action, so that in time you will be able to give, as well as to receive, and to create environments for yourself and for others, even when they are lacking.

But quite apart from the ethical importance of the color sense, its development has such a practical bearing on our work, our homes, public buildings, gardens, apparel, and relationships, in short, on everything that makes life dignified, lovable, and profitable, that we cannot afford to remain in ignorance of all the benefits that its scientific understanding will confer upon us. Rally, therefore, color students; rally to this great cause, and speed its coming with your utmost endeavor and generosity!

CHAPTER X COLOR STIMULI AND EXERCISES

Though this little work is primarily an appeal for a color theater and a color college, the writer is well aware that such institutions can only be securely and justly founded upon the aggregate initiative of the sincere lovers of chromatology.

And it will be owing to their collective study and endeavor, rather than to my individual vision, that the color edifices of the near future will become accomplished facts.

It is my enthusiast's hope that all the readers of these notes will consider it worth while to give chromatology a serious consideration, for it is not with the object of pleasing sensation-mongers, nor of launching an aesthetic "novelty," that the propositions contained in this book have been set forth.

The question that will naturally occur to all inquirers is, but how can one commence this study of color without a guide or rules?

My reply to that is, that before being in a position to even commence studies, the color sense must be tested and quickened to a degree which will form a startingpoint. One does not attempt to make an infant walk before his muscles can stand the strain, and the candidate for color development must have the humility of a child and the ambition of an athlete, if he is going to succeed in his quest. The study of color in nature should be the student's I first step.

A few words upon the pagan emulation of physical beauty and culture seem to me *apropos* in this connection. It is sad that a degeneracy in its devotees should have exposed to misunderstanding a cult, which was originally inspired by ideals of selfdiscipline and self-sacrifice, and which had a deep, spiritual significance in the wellbeing of the State. For how could the sculpture and tradition of the ancients have exercised the profound influence that it has done, had it been otherwise?

It is to be desired, then, that the cult of chromatology shall have its mainspring in similar ideals, and that its development shall confer the same lifegiving benefits upon the State. The new science of color will provide psychic instead of physical culture.

The history of national thought, and the ultimate purpose of our own senses, those dominant actors in the drama of life, alike testify that spiritual awakening is caused in the first instance by an indefinable appreciation of a fresh source of beauty. In many cases this beauty is not apparent to anyone but ourselves, and though its message may in a measure sever us physically and mentally from the world for a short time, yet eventually it unites us spiritually to our fellow-creatures, and gives us a sense of kinship with the whole of existence that was undreamed of before. In this newfound freedom, we experience the exclusive pride of potentates, mingled with an overflowing generosity that knows itself the possessor of inexhaustible treasures.

When the color sense has been quickened through nature studies to this point of universal appreciation, the first step has been taken, but not till then should the student commence work in earnest. The next important point is to construct a color chart, or to verify mine. This done, you are in a position to select the branch of chromatology through which you intend to achieve your color development and in which you wish to excel.

Finally, experiment and *observe* without ceasing. This general advice as to the best method of making a start can be quite specifically used, but it is well to remember that chromatology is a long and profound study, and that you had better leave it alone unless you are prepared to be patient and to win your way slowly into the heart of its shining mysteries.

If you avail yourself intelligently of these broad principles contained in this book, they will open out wider vistas of research and experiment, by means of which you can make individual discoveries. At the present stage of evolution, both in this science and in ourselves, it is, however, essential to regard the first aim of chromatology as an individual unfoldment for the sake of the betterment and service of the race. And it is safe to assert that any student who approaches this science in a small spirit will obtain small results from his labors, and will remain a dweller in the outer courts of its wisdom.

Yet even individual egotism cannot thwart the working of the law, for any degree of color development, no matter how small, quickens the creature, and makes him a more vital member of the community.

In choosing a branch of chromatology, one should be careful to select that one most suited to one's temperament and circumstances. The area of choice is sufficiently wide to meet all requirement, for, as I have shown, chromatology includes aesthetic expressions, healing, social reform, and last, but not necessarily least, personal development.

If your life is absorbed in social duties, do not attempt to become a color healer, or a reformer, for the austere conditions necessary for development in these branches would be incompatible with your environment.

In such a case it would be wiser to devote yourself to some aesthetic medium of expression, such as painting, or color production through sound, either in speaking or singing, or you could concentrate on a personal development dominated by impersonal motives.

Indeed, one cannot too strenuously cultivate this spirit of impersonality, or, more correctly speaking, universality, for before it obstacles vanish from the path of the seeker, and it matters little through what channel he advances on the rainbow road of color, provided he preserves a receptive and tolerant attitude, and a respectful recognition of the fact that all roads lead eventually to the mountain top. A person may call himself a chromatologist from that moment in which he learns to liberate and to recognize himself in the larger scheme of nature, and to pulse in unison with her multi-colored breast.

When he can do this by means of concentrating on any color in the landscape until he has received its message, then he will understand the real point of departure more profoundly than any words of mine can convey it.

And now let us consider the minor color stimuli at our disposal in this quest.

These fall under two heads, *i. e.,* personal experiment, and the analysis of experiments already made for us by others.

Personal experiment contains endless possibilities, and if I only cite a few elementary tests, it is because I wish you to evolve more complex problems of your own.

One simple exercise is to try the effect of different environments upon yourself and upon others.

Surround yourself, at first, actually, and when you are more developed, mentally, with the color waves whose life you wish to test and understand.

Another good method is to study the

action of color upon children and animals and, if you have a garden, the effect of colored shrubs upon yourself.

A subtler stimulus than either of the preceding lies in the endeavor to correlate sound and perfume with color. This is an excellent experiment, but it must be made with great care, and in as negative a frame of mind as possible, otherwise one's intellect is apt to suggest spurious correspondences.

You can carry out this test in the following manner: Concentrate your attention upon a sound or a perfume, considering it as a complete and detached expression in itself. After a time you will find that some color will imperceptibly pervade your consciousness, at first so faintly, so subtly, that you perceive it only as an intensified appreciation of the sound or the perfume.

Gradually this increased tension relaxed and your perception becomes slightly blurred, like a landscape that softens at sunrise. This relaxation develops into an expansion from which the perception of a definite color emanates. That color is for you the correspondence of the note or perfume upon which you concentrated.

The reason why no two people would ever get quite the same correspondence is that no two organisms vibrate habitually alike, though they may do so occasionally, under exceptional circumstances. This does not alter the fact that an absolute correspondence does exist between color, sound, and perfume, and the more sensitive a person is, the nearer will their color perception be to the actual correspondence.

The achievement of this experiment simply means that by an effort of concentration we have keyed ourselves to a pitch at which we can apprehend, more or less correctly, the triple vibration which is an essential condition of sound, color, and perfume; or in other words, we apprehend the synthetic life of each of these manifestations simultaneously.

Conversely, we can extract from color its sound and its perfume, but this is a much more difficult matter and one that requires a finer adjustment of vibrations.

These are only a few of the experiments that can be made, but they are fundamentally useful, because the vitality that they confer upon the color sense can be expended later on whatever branch of chromatology we elect to specialize in.

Concerning the experiments that have been made for us, and to which I have already referred in a previous chapter, they are numerous, and have been recorded in written works which are at the student's disposal in any library. To quote just a few: there are Professor Schellen's *Spectrum Analysis,* Preston's *Theory of Light,* Dr. Kilner's *Human Atmosphere,* Dr. Gr. MacDonald's *Sound and Color, Music and Morals,* by Haweis, Professor Tyndall's paper on "Light," Helmholtz's *Sensations of Tone,* and *Color-Music,* by Wallace Eimington. Locke and Nussbaum have written on "color-hearing"; Rimbaud, the French poet, has developed a "color theory." Arthur Mitzscherling, the psychologist, has discussed the ethical and sensory value of color; and Schopenhauer,' the philosopher, has also dealt with the same subject at some length. The American scientist, E. Mount Bleyer, has contributed pamphlets on the relation existing between color and sound. He has also patented an instrument called the "vibrograph," by means of which he has proved that each sound has a corresponding form, in the case of single notes, geometric symbols, while harmonic arrangements often produce designs resembling beautiful vegetable and sea-growths.

These experiments are discussed at length in Dr. Bleyer's pamphlets, and proving as they do, the synthetic life of sound and color, they form an eloquent appeal for chromatology.

Another interesting test that has been made for us is the "color organ" built by Professor Rimington and described fully in his book, *Color-Music.* Through the medium of his color organ, Professor Rimington originates what he calls, the "art of mobile color.'' This art has already contributed some data upon the powers of color, and it is to be hoped that Professor Eimington will place the benefits of these experiments within the reach of wider recognition.

Die Farben Kurven bei Reduktion auf gleiche Helligkeit. Die Welt als Wille und Vorstellung.

Mr. William Fraetas, of Maitland, Cape Town, one of the most advanced workers in the color cause, has formulated a "color law," whose technical application for scientific training he is now completing; and though Mr. Fraetas has not explained his "system" to me, an interesting conversation with him leads me to believe that his "color law" may prove a valuable asset to the color college of the future.

In New York (1910) and in London (1912), I made some public color experiments myself of an elementary nature, for details of which I refer the reader to the Appendix.

These demonstrations for testing the effect of certain luminous masses of color were given in the form of aesthetic entertainments, which " I called "Color-poemevenings. ''

Notwithstanding some bewilderment and conflicting criticisms, my little venture met with a most encouraging response from press and public, and, had there been sufficient capital in hand, I would have given a series of free demonstrations, for to the unprepared mind the truths of this revelation will have to be abundantly and circumstantially illustrated before they can meet with attention, much less respect.

At the Hudson Theater in New York, where my name was already familiar to the public in connection with the production of poetic plays, one of my chief obstacles lay in the difficulty that I had in getting people to disassociate my known personality from this new work, and to realize that the "color-poem-evening" was something more than an entertainment, and that beneath its aesthetic appeal there lay a scientific and philosophic message.

When, therefore, I gave the demonstrations in London (May, 1912, Crosby Hall), to combat this misunderstanding, and at the suggestion of several persons interested in the work, I annexed a "Foreword" to my program, in which I stated the aims of my experiment. This foreword is also at the reader's disposal in the Appendix, though it is but a cursory synopsis of an important aesthetic aspect of chromatology.

CHAPTER XI COLOR-SCIENCE AND INTERIOR DECORATION

Possibly one of the most practical and universal channels through which color-science can and will work is through the art of interior decoration. The hygienic and the aesthetic significance of color will be gradually but surely demonstrated through its discriminating and scientific use in our homes; and since environment plays an important part in the development of our color sense, we can sensitize ourselves to receive the messages of color by having it harmoniously and abundantly expressed in our surroundings.

The art of interior decoration will gain a new and a deeper significance through its alliance with color-science, which, in its turn, will owe much to this intimate channel of personal appeal and experiment.

The desire for individual expression and experiment in the home is increasing, and, without exaggeration, one may say that the manipulation of color is the main object of modern decoration, while the slavish reproduction of certain "periods," such as "Louis XV.," etc., is being relegated to overstocked furniture warehouses, and to the service of people who have more money than individuality.

In the course of this chapter I will show how, through the aid of color-science as applied to decoration and chiefly to illumination, one room may be redecorated seven times a week, or even seven times a day, without any outlay, except the initial outlay of taste and knowledge.

The Japanese have an excellent idea of never exhibiting more than one object of beauty in a room at a time, but in the case of people who have collections of art treasures, this object is changed daily.

By such a system, taste is not degenerated through a multiplicity of impressions, yet the mind is constantly re-freshed with new visions. If we adapt the underlying philosophy of this method to the art of decoration, we shall bring about a new type of environment, in which our own thought and feeling will have room to expand and to express itself.

If our rooms are replete with created images of other people's brains, how can our own imagination have its nec-essary play? The scientific use of color will provide a stimulus, without creat-ing the didactic limitations that are im-posed by conventional designs.

One may say that the message of col-or or light first made itself felt through an increasing demand for ventilation and luminosity. Compare the lofty and numerous windows of modern struc-tures with the narrow, slit-like aper-tures, scarcely more than peep-holes, that served our ancestors in castle and cottage alike, and we shall be obliged to confess that it took some time before the race realized even the physical mes-sages of light and their accruing ben-efits. Similarly, the psychic and philo-sophical messages of color will be grad-ually made manifest through these uni-versal and essential institutions of the home, and of the public buildings in which we seek the larger life that re-cre-ates our thought and enriches our per-sonal viewpoint. A cosmopolitan obser-vation has convinced me that the art of interior decoration suffers from three limitations or conditions, which the knowledge of color-science would go far to remove.

These obstructive conditions might be classified under the terms of incon-gruity, irrelevancy, and stolidity. Let me try to explain these charges, lest I be condemned as an arrogant enthusiast, unjust to past and present, and with vi-sion only for a future that lies too far ahead to be of material significance.

Individual taste expresses itself here and there with a sincerity that is the more striking by reason of its isolation; but, on the whole, buildings in the West, both externally and internally, are in-clined to be incongruous because they do not harmonize with either the land-

scape or the climate; irrelevant, because they have no intimate correspondence with the people who frequent them; and stolid, because the development of their detail is based upon a low standard of utility—the highest standard of utility always including a regard for beauty, which satisfies man's greater as well as his lesser needs.

It is not mere pretension that urges us to a display of brilliance in our recep-tion rooms, and to a restful luxuriance in our bedrooms, but it is the underlying fact that in the former conditions we de-sire to express our minds, in the latter to renew our bodies.

It is from dearth that "we discover and create new laws, and, therefore, I venture to predict that in the future dec-orative art will be more influenced by the observance of congruity, relevancy, and beauty, than it has been in the past, and that the individual as well as the ex-pert will study his responsibilities upon these points.

Then we shall no longer see Eastern architecture under Western skies, nor will romantic retreats be disfigured by cheap cottages and villas whose defi-ciencies are only accentuated by na-ture's exquisite rhythms.

It is not necessary for an edifice to be costly to insure its harmony, but it is necessary that it should establish its relation coherently and profoundly with its location, its occupants, and with beauty.

Two other points that have always struck me as oppressive in interior dec-oration were the disposition of artificial lights and the heterogenous collections of art objects with which people delight to obliterate every vista of space and shadow. Decorative art has still much to learn from elimination and from illumi-nation.

It is an astonishing fact that many people who collect beautiful things have so little knowledge of how to re-spect their possessions, or to display them to advantage. I have seen glowing porcelains and pictures almost obliter-ated by indiscriminate association with objects of a coarser vibration. It is not the collection but the collector that is at

fault. One cannot have too many trea-sures, but the manner of their exhibition should preoccupy us more. I am sure that until we understand the decorative value of space and shadow, also their relation to color, vitally harmonious in-teriors cannot be created.

This consideration brings us to the all-important problem of illumination. The use of indirect and shaded lighting, though not yet universal, has gone far to remedy the fatiguing effect of direct masses or spots of light; but color-sci-ence will enable us to evolve a luminous system that will not only be more deco-rative in character, but one that will co-operate more intimately and efficiently with our environments, and free them to a great extent of their present stolidity.

It is an unnatural condition that man, whose organism is mobile and irides-cent, should dwell in a fixity of any one form or color.

For most of us, the cost of constant redecoration is prohibitive, but through a knowledge of color-science, and the application of its principles to illumina-tion, we shall obviate much of the mo-notony that causes depression.

One of the secrets of our pleasure and well-being, when we are out of doors, lies in the fact that we are enfolded in the ever-changing vibrations of nature's multicolored breast. The greatest use in-variably underlies the greatest beauty, which is an axiom that can be proved by experiment, paradoxical as it may sound.

There is no valid reason for the con-ventional positions generally assigned to lighting fixtures, and on general prin-ciples it is only in the dining-room and banqueting hall that a central and uni-versal system of lighting is desirable, because in such rooms it is essential, and in conformity with the uses of that room.

In reception rooms, whose purpose is sociability and variety, light could be more vitally used were it reflected at in-tervals, in pools, in the floor, each pool being capable of changing color if desir-able.

In ballrooms there is a particularly wide scope for novelty and improvement. Luminous glass floors, combined with a discreet side lighting, would give a better result than has yet been achieved, for it is in the rhythmic feet and bodies, not in the flushed faces, that the beauty of the ballroom lies. Added to this, any heat overhead is trying to a sensitive dancer. I throw out these suggestions to illustrate what refreshing results the art of lighting will achieve when it shall become intelligently allied to colorscience. Then, illumination will no longer be mechanical, or the outcome of mechanical minds, but it will be a power, capable of enveloping us in an atmospheric mobility that will vie with nature's reviving and everchanging color schemes.

An entire volume could be written on color correspondence in relation to interior decoration, and it is my purpose to publish such a work at no distant date. Meanwhile, I must ask indulgence for a very cursory treatment of an important subject, and for the enunciation of general principles only.

Halls and entrances, instead of being somber, should radiate recuperative or stimulant colors. Sedative or recuperative tints are most suitable for diningrooms, stimulant colors for reception rooms, and recuperative and sedative schemes for bedrooms. The most important point to observe, however, is that every surrounding should meet the individual requirements of the person who owns it.

Until the scientific color principles that should underlie decoration become more widely diffused, this new art could receive vital assistance from the color theater, upon whose luminous prosceniums could be flashed series of color combinations that had been worked out by experts, for schemes of decoration, and from which the onlooker could make his choice.

In conclusion, I should like to put forward a plea for a device that could well be included in every house, since its use would hasten the development that would eventually make the individual his own adviser upon all questions pertaining to color.

In the home, some room, or even an alcove, might be dedicated to color alone. Such a retreat should, if possible, be circular in shape, devoid of furniture, save for a couch or cushions, and the draperies that composed its walls should comprise curtains of varying tones and textures that could be intermingled by a system of pulleys. In such a retreat, regardless of season and circumstance, the individual could enfold himself at will in the greens of the forest, the purple of the sea, the azure of heaven, or the soft fawns and umbers of the earth, and he could gradually derive from each color the message that would satisfy his needs.

CHAPTER XII THE COLOR AGE AND COLOR DBAMA

In concluding this short brief for the "science of color," I should like to suggest a few thoughts upon the universal aspect of the question.

All science is man's answer, more or less imperfect, to man's needs. It is the eternally budding tree of knowledge, the choice immortelle of evolution, for its blossom and its fruit endure through countless changing forms that are fashioned to meet the requirements of the century from which it springs. And though at first glance science may appear to be the independent offspring of a few advanced thinkers, this is not in reality the case, for science is only the rational and necessary answer to the aggregate need.

A clear vision, and the voicing of it, may be granted to a few men in advance if their development is such as to render them a reliable mouthpiece for truth; but more than spokesmen they are not, for what they think and utter, their fellowmen are already feeling and seeking an explanation of, in a manner that is often confused owing to its very intensity.

This fact accounts for the storm of contradiction and ridicule that assails the lonely bearers of new light, but that is an inevitable test. If the speakers are genuine bearers of the sacred fire, their voices may be drowned for a while, but not silenced, their light scorned, but not extinguished.

And if chromatology is to take a place beside her shining sister sciences, she cannot escape the ordeals that they have had to undergo.

If she could do so, she would not be worthy to clasp hands with them, and no less than theirs, can her destined evolution and recognition be retarded one hairbreadth by any unjust opposition.

The chosen ones will speak when the need of their fellow-men cries aloud; those very men who insist that, as a proof of its worth, the thing which they desire shall outlive the coarse laugh, the cynical smile, the cold indifference, and the brutal hatred and envy of all the outworn creeds that rise up to crush it.

Not until truth has survived these superhuman tests, is she cherished and honored by the sons of men.

And why should it be otherwise? Each formula of truth is purchased at such a cost, that it cannot lightly be set aside, no matter how threadbare it has become. Humanity clings to the faded garment until (delicious irony) it is scattered in fragments by the blast of its own righteous indignation at the sight of new apparel! When his need is stark, man accepts the fair raiment, but not sooner, and chromatology must wait her appointed hour, submissive but serene in knowledge of her wealth.

Now, if we take a rapid survey of existing conditions, we shall find that they justify the claim of this new science to be an answer to many modern demands.

Let us first consider in what degree chromatology can be regarded as a necessary answer to a universal need, which is already expressed through other scientific manifestations of a more practical, but *not* more essential nature.

If we reflect on the trend of modern civilization, we must be forcibly struck by two facts, namely, that all its manifestations are devoted to the expression of speed, and that the partial achievement of this speed ideal, having revolutionized and co-ordinated our outer life, is now proceeding to influence our personal intercourse.

In external communication, railways, motors, and aviation are reducing the problems of time and space, and linking the interests of countries that a century ago were unknown to each other. Then there is the cinematograph, which binds the wonders of nature and the events of progress all over the world into one amazing volume accessible to all readers.

Besides the cinematograph, which puts us in telepathic touch with the doings of the universe, we have those more intimate inventions of wireless telegraphy, wireless telephone, telephone, and Esperanto, the universal language.

The aim of all these contrivances is speed; in fact, the world seems bound for some new goal to which these inventions are but signposts. And what is this dim beauty towards which we are straining? Possibly, indeed probably, it is the dawn of a telepathic and color era, on whose threshold we are now standing, clamorous with a thousand conflicting tongues, and somewhat bewildered by the new light that is flooding our planet, and that is dazzling us with its unaccustomed strength.

We are approaching an age of mental telepathy, in which the organism of the race is about to become attuned to the second sense of the earth and to the third element that sustains her, *i. e.,* air, and in which our action and outlook will alike assume the characteristics of that element, which are elasticity and brilliance. I believe that aviation only marks the beginning of our connection with this unexplored range of forces.

But in the noonday of this telepathic era, color will be a recognized force, just as much as electricity and sound are now; it will be used for healing of body and development of mind, it will be found to possess the same philosophical and ethical value as music, and in due course it may possibly become our medium of personal communication.

Speech may be replaced by a color code, our intercourse will be literally illumined, and we shall look back upon words with the same pitying, amused smile as that which we would now bestow on the cave drawings of a primitive race.

Which one of us has not experienced moments when speech, either written or spoken, was wholly inadequate to convey the vibrations of life with which he found himself overflowing?

In such moments we were dimly aware of our color systems, but as our organisms evolve, these momentary expansions will increase in frequency and in intensity until we extract a new coherence from them.

Already numbers of people, and among them prominent scientific men, have brought ordinary telepathy to an advanced stage as a method of inquiry into the nature of thought waves and etheric sensibility. There can be no doubt that these side issues are paving the way to the telepathic color era, but in spite of their service our unrest calls for a more intimate appeal and assurance.

Our brains are busy with this color-science, but as yet our hearts have not been touched, and therefore the result of our research has been somewhat meager. Unconvinced as yet of color's essential relation to our existence, we have only succeeded in dimly discerning the purpose of her existence, but of her life-giving rhythms few can speak with faith, much less with authority. The question then arises, How can this general apathy and individual doubt be dispelled? For we must inevitably return to the axiom that the aggregate need calls forth the necessary answer. At this juncture the best manner therefore of assisting individual workers to conclusions would appear to lie in giving a stimulus to general inquiry.

Now history shows that the *social* application of new sciences or trends of thought is generally brought about by the Church or the theater, sometimes by both.

These institutions invoke the higher imaginative faculties, through which truth is more readily apprehended by the average brain, and they also have a sentimental hold upon general beliefs and inclinations.

For this reason, in primitive times, the drama was the foundling of the Church, and even if civilization had lured her far afield, she is none the less imbued with the characteristics of her first associations and *au fond* she remains a handmaiden whose destiny it is to carry the temple lamp into the marketplace.

In reference to the mysteries of color, it seems to me that we have reached a point at which we await the voice of religion or drama, or both, to confirm to our hearts what our heads are already analyzing.

Many indirect forecasts have been made, but we need some definite statement to inspire our enthusiasm and illumine our vision. I venture to believe that this statement and impetus can alone be supplied by the dignified foundation of a color theater.

About two years ago, Israel Zangwill published a play called *The New Religion,* in which he foreshadowed a formula of faith based upon a combination of scientific certainty and aesthetic beauty, and on such a faith as this the color institutions of the future will be founded.

Another indirect forecast on the ultimate recognition of color as a universal necessity has reached us through the tenets of the Bahai movement, that splendid religious and scientific philosophy which had its inception in Persia seventy years ago, and which now numbers a following of over ten thousand souls in the western hemisphere and over one million in the land of its birth.

This movement, standing as it does for a synthetic expression of religion with science and social organism, is replacing the voice of the Orthodox Church, heralding an era of spiritual telepathy and universal religious tolerance, and it is urging the development of *all* sciences, trades, and arts that can conduce to a closer brotherhood among men and to a higher efficiency of the race.

It is obvious that such an expanded and inclusive revelation of truth is highly propitious to the future of chromatology, and when the Bahai teachings are more widely known and practiced, the uses of color will also be better understood; because the etherealization of inner conditions results in an etheralization of outer expressions. This spiritual or complete realization, however, will only mark the final developments of chromatology. Meanwhile, we are only facing towards the dawn of this science.

Once we have grasped a thing mentally, our next effort is directed to the experimental use of our knowledge through sensory mediums, and so we find that already the theater has been lisping the color message in monosyllables. She is fashioning fair forms through which we shall grow to love this new science and to demand of it all the powers and the pleasures that it can bestow on us.

Vide *The Reconciliation of Races and religions,* Professor Cheyne; *The Modern Social Religion,* Horace Holley; *L'£pitre au Fils du Loup,* Hippolyte Dreyfus.

In 1910, Charles Urban's colored films, representing the birth and growth of flowers in all their subtle gradations of tint, were the real beginnings of chromatology in the theater, and since then the cinematograph has evolved the expression of color considerably. In other theaters the plays that have been most successful within the last five years are those that have lent themselves to feasts, sometimes, alas, orgies of color. *Sumurun, Kismet, Belladonna* were successively the rage, to say nothing of Granville Barker's vivid Shakespearean productions.

The cinematograph, however, is the true forerunner, for in its abolition of words and development of color, it has introduced us crudely to the new drama of the telepathic era, which will be known as the color drama.

The abolition of words will probably be followed by the abolition of scenery, and we shall wonder how we could ever have been encumbered with either one or the other.

The dramatic expression of chromatology will be one of the most practical and powerful manifestations of the new science, for it will demonstrate the ethical value of color, and attract people to the study of its deeper issues, just as the literary drama has caused people to study literature and the various problems which have been raised by thoughtful plays.

But this color drama will be able to handle the old problems, and new ones of its own making, and it will create new industries, textile, electric, and chemical, and fresh visions, pleasures, and perceptions for us.

At first these dramas may be accompanied by the wordless action of some story that will lend itself to a dramatic color exposition, but gradually stories will go the way of words and scenery, and colors will be the only and triumphant *dramatis personae!* They will clash and merge before us in a subtler concourse than any we have hitherto known, and we shall find a response to their language in our own etherealized equations.

The temples of this telepathic color drama will be built in pale marbles, relieved with onyx, ebony, and granite; they will be devoid of gilding or ornament save that afforded by luminous fretworks of alabaster, and aluminum, and an aesthetic disposition of sunken colored lights, whose reflections will play upon cornices that are too hard or shadows that are too heavy! The whole cool, gleaming auditorium will echo but relieve the glowing proscenium, so that the spectator may be enveloped in a continuous atmosphere of true and harmonic color vibrations.

The stage will be fitted with hanging draperies that can be raised or lowered in the same way that scenery is now handled.

These draperies will be of differing textures and tone, but mostly pale in tint, and over them in endless waves, color will flow from electric claviers that will be highly evolved mobile editions of the present switch boards, arc lamps, etc.

, These waves of color will closely follow the action of the drama, and will reveal it with a suggestive poignance far surpassing the inanimate objective environments to which we have hitherto been accustomed.

Even in the limited scope of my little experiment, and with only the present primitive color resources available, I was astonished at the response that my color scheme met with.

What could one not accomplish if adequate resources were forthcoming for large productions on the lines that I have indicated? Surely this is a vision beautiful enough to inspire the co-operative endeavor of all color students and the generosity of the most advanced philanthropists. Why should there be any long waiting for the realization of a color theater when so much material lies ready for production? One color drama with a full orchestral accompaniment is completed, and there are others in the making.

Science also has labeled many of the functions of color for us, and our gratitude and respect are due to her research; but these labeled functions are scattered on different laboratory shelves, where they are crying aloud for cohesion into *one* body, whose powers, latent and expressed, shall be synchronized and given forth to a waiting world.

Surely, then, it is incumbent on the awakened ones to hasten the recognition of this science with all their might, for not until philanthropy, art, and science have transmuted this message and adjusted its several parts into a living organism, can it go forth conquering, arrayed in the light of the telepathic color age, and equipped to flash all its messages into the heart of the expectant race.

COLOR-POEM RECITALS BY BEATRICE IRWIN

NEW.YORK

Herald.—"Beatrice Irwin, attired in attractive costumes, most of them suggestive of the Orient, posed against scenic backgrounds as she declaimed her color-poems, while ever-changing colored lights were thrown upon her." *Globe.*— "The settings designed by Miss Irwin were exquisite and really showed a fine sense of colorharmony." *Times.*—"Miss Irwin made a very difficult and delicate experiment. Her aim is spiritual suggestion through the mysterious medium of color." LONDON *World.*—"Miss Beatrice Irwin, who has already won deserving recognition as one of the most gifted of our younger poets, revealed exceptional talent of another order a few evenings ago at Crosby Hall, where her rendering of her *Color-Poems* made a marked impression upon a deeply-interested audience." *Queen.*—"Miss Beatrice Irwin presented exquisite pictures of form and color, and her movements and expression were everything that could be desired. Her color schemes were wonderfully thought out, and her costumes beautiful in their poetical symbolism."

Given at the

Hudson Theatre, Friday, November 18th, 1910

Program i. Utro PaFttta

Cyrus, My Peacock

A Persian with her peacock

The Chinese Rain-Bird

Which heralds the storm Meadow Larks

Which herald Dawn

The Dragon-Fish-Bird

An Aeroplane ode ii. ©rietttal flioe-ma

Tsune, from Kioto

Where the Past lingers on rare Kake-monas Hai-Lin, a Flower Girl from Canton The Music of Japan Heard through the April dusk, white with rain of falling blossoms The Flute—*played by the blind masseur* The Samisen—*by frail Musmes* The Koto—*by the Court musician* The Temple Gong—*sounded by the priest to invoke Buddha's blessing and to call pilgrims to prayer* in. ij-janoalalt, (\$uwti of thf Ponoaa

An African tribe that holds the Mamba serpent sacred to the souls of their Chiefs iv. Arifttijon, from Athena

The eternal mourner for Beauty IN-TERVAL v. &0tt90 of % lElrottttte

Rain-Rhythms

Earth-Worship

Air-Echoes

Sea-Love

Fire-Myths VI. Ittatttfl Of % *BtBStt*

Where Sun and Silence merge

Vii. £nt» *\$atma*

The Siren

(500b.c.)

Fan-Poem

Moon-Dance

Beloved

Fuchsia

Bezito

Spikenard written by BEATRICE IR-WIN and recited by her in Costume and Setting

Incidental accompaniment by VAN RENSSELAER SHIEL FOREWORD TO PRO-GRAM Given at

Crosby Hall, London, May 21, 1912

I Come before you to demonstrate the art of geometric harmony, or triple vibration, through the expressed correspondences of form, color, and sound.

This art was studied by the ancients for the purpose of increasing vitality, and of obtaining aesthetic pleasure.

The actual correspondences now existing between form, color, and sound are now a matter of scientific fact, and Dr. Mount Bleyer's instrument, the vibrograph, has registered in *Tone Pictures* the geometric forms of sound.

In the same manner that a note sung or spoken through the vibrograph, onto a powdered membrane, leaves its symbol upon the membrane, so the simultaneous expression of corresponding forms, colors, and sounds can, by their vibrations, create symbols upon the elastic membrane of the atmosphere, and these symbols react upon those in their vicinity.

Poetry, being a formula of concentrated vitality, is a very suitable medium for the demonstration of geometric harmony, as the words it employs have more creative sound-force than the words of ordinary usage.

My little book, *The Pagan Trinity,* is

only, as it were, a primer of geometric harmony, but in subject and treatment it is concerned with the primal rhythm of substances, with the color of rhythms.

The open-air theater of the ancients, with its subtle chiaroscuro of atmospheric effects, and the chanting measure of their verse, witnesses to a profound knowledge of the fact that by attuning human passion to the passion of nature a sublime vigor could be acquired as well as imparted.

Therefore, with a suggestive reproduction of nature's color waves, and with the limited equipment that individual effort permits, I venture to place my work before you, hoping to reach and rest you.

BEATRICE IRWIN.

At Crosby Hall, London *Impromptu* .. .. Gabriel Faure Mario Lorenzi i. Ofy *Wt'wxt* (Where Color dreams)

Petals

The Music of Japan *(Flute, Samisen, Koto, and Temple Gong)*

Fan Poem *(after the manner of the Chinese) Nordische Ballade...* Franz Poenitz

Mario Lorenzi II. Nature WnrHljtp (On the four altars of Sound)

Rain-Rhythms

E arth-Worship

Air-Ecstasy

Sea-Love

Fire-Myth *Gigue* ...... Mario Lorenzi *Arabesque* ...... Debussy

Mario Lorenzi in. Iwama of % *Btsttt* (Where Form springs from Silence)

The Eternal Idol

Dawn

Song of the Desert, and Song of the Sun iv. Atriatum (The new Rhythm)

The Dragon-Fish-Bird

Icarus

CPSIA information can be obtained
at www.ICGtesting.com
Printed in the USA
LVOW04s2313280717
543066LV00003B/54/P